"The black darkness of the sky,

the stars twinkling above, and

hour after hour going by with

no sunlight. Every now and then

a moon when storms do not

come, and always the cold,

getting colder and colder..."

—Matthew Henson

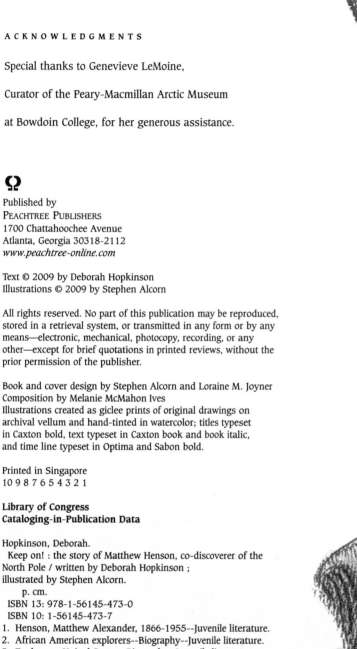

For Deborah Wiles, a true friend on this journey and always there to haul me out of holes.

—D. H.

For Leo, loyal sleigh-riding companion of my youth.

—S. A

ACKNOWLEDGMENTS

Special thanks to Genevieve LeMoine,

Curator of the Peary-Macmillan Arctic Museum

at Bowdoin College, for her generous assistance.

Published by
PEACHTREE PUBLISHERS
1700 Chattahoochee Avenue
Atlanta, Georgia 30318-2112
www.peachtree-online.com

Text © 2009 by Deborah Hopkinson
Illustrations © 2009 by Stephen Alcorn

Book and cover design by Stephen Alcorn and Loraine M. Joyner
Composition by Melanie McMahon Ives
Illustrations created as giclee prints of original drawings on archival vellum and hand-tinted in watercolor; titles typeset in Caxton bold, text typeset in Caxton book and book italic, and time line typeset in Optima and Sabon bold.

Printed in Singapore
10 9 8 7 6 5 4 3 2 1

Library of Congress
Cataloging-in-Publication Data

Hopkinson, Deborah.
  Keep on! : the story of Matthew Henson, co-discoverer of the North Pole / written by Deborah Hopkinson ;
illustrated by Stephen Alcorn.
    p. cm.
  ISBN 13: 978-1-56145-473-0
  ISBN 10: 1-56145-473-7
  1. Henson, Matthew Alexander, 1866-1955--Juvenile literature.
  2. African American explorers--Biography--Juvenile literature.
  3. Explorers--United States--Biography--Juvenile literature.
  4. North Pole--Discovery and exploration--Juvenile literature.
  5. Arctic regions--Discovery and exploration--Juvenile
literature. I. Alcorn, Stephen, ill. II. Title.
  G635.H4H67 2009
  910.911'3--dc22
          2008031118

The text of KEEP ON! is based on primary and secondary sources. Every attempt has been made to verify the information contained within, and any errors are the responsibility of the author. The artwork is inspired by the text and is a creative interpretation of the events described.

Keep On!

THE STORY OF

Matthew Henson

CO-DISCOVERER OF THE

North Pole

written by
deborah hopkinson

illustrated by
stephen alcorn

PEACHTREE
ATLANTA

MATTHEW HENSON

was born in a Maryland cabin,

at a time when boys dreamed of finding glory,

of planting flags at the ends of the Earth,

making the unknown known,

and recording their names into history books.

Young Matt had that same hunger to explore,

but most folks would have laughed at his dreams.

For Matt was born in 1866, just after the Civil War,

a time when poor black boys like him

had few chances to roam the next county,

to say nothing of another country, the seven seas,

or the top of the world.

By the time he was thirteen, Matt was alone.

He set out to make his way in the world,

trudging the long road from Washington, D.C.,

to the harbor of Baltimore.

What a bustling place it was!

Gulls screeched;

men shouted and rushed about,

loading and unloading ships of every size.

And Matt stood alone, keen as an Arctic fox,

eager to pounce on any chance he could find.

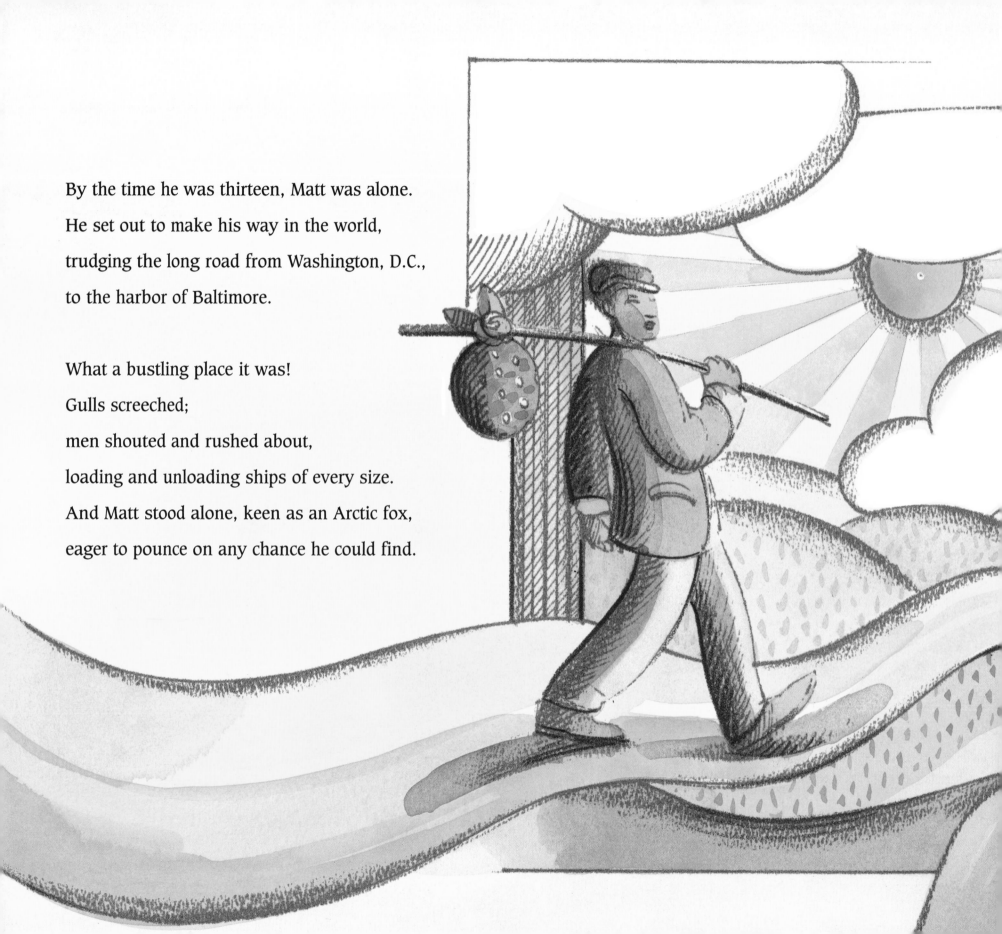

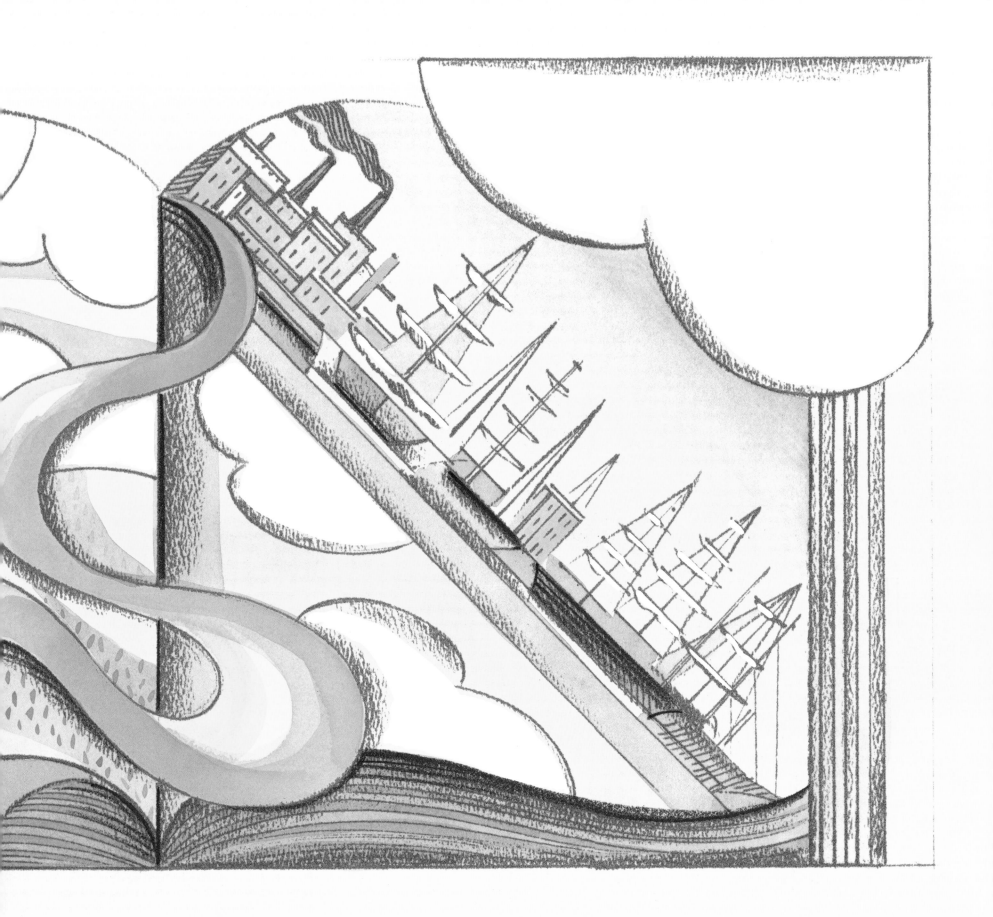

"I shipped as cabin-boy, on board a vessel bound for China. After my first voyage...I became an able-bodied seaman...sailing to China, Japan...North Africa, Spain, France, and through the Black Sea to Southern Russia."

Matt spied the *Katie Hines*,

a three-masted vessel so sharp and bright,

she seemed like a star gliding on water.

And when he spotted her proud,

　white-haired captain,

Matt begged for a chance to go to sea.

It was breaking the rules to let a boy

　under fifteen sail,

but that old sea dog took a liking to him,

and Matthew Alexander Henson became

　his cabin boy.

For the next five years,

Matt's school was the world,

his classroom the boat.

Captain Childs taught him history and mathematics,

and soon Matt could navigate by the stars,

    tie sailor's knots,

and fix or build most anything.

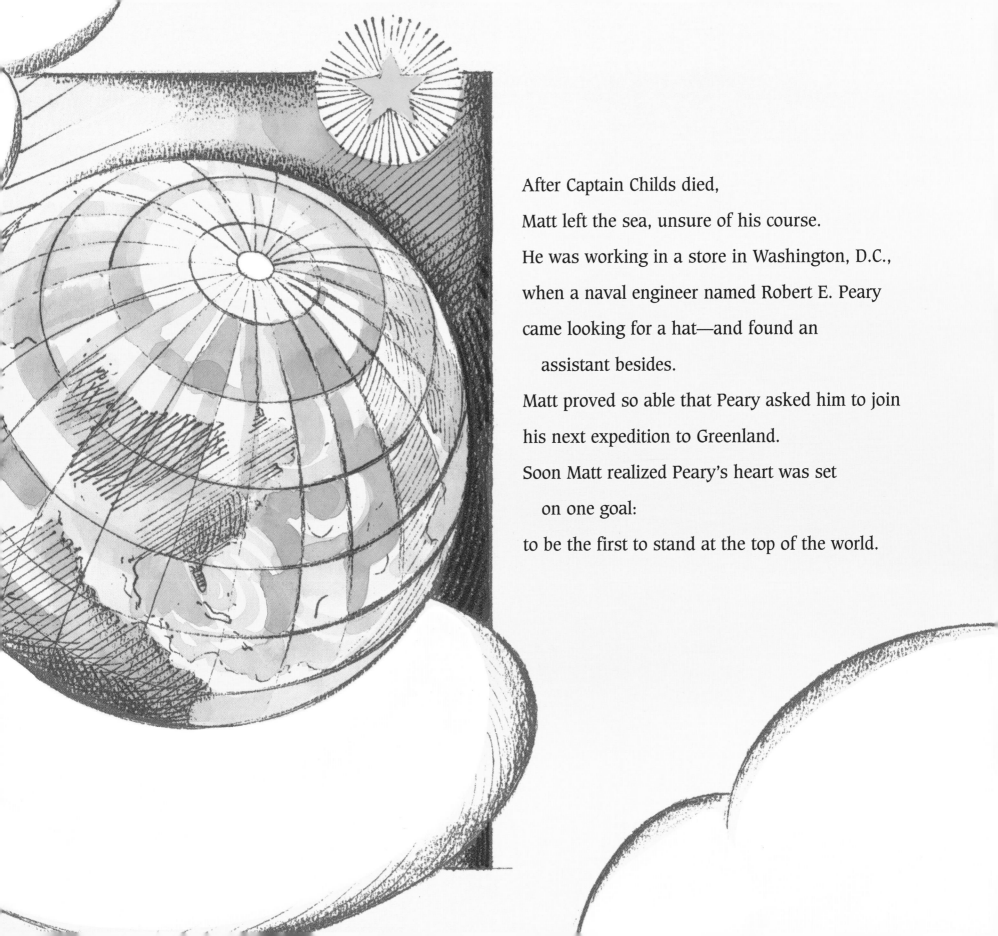

After Captain Childs died,

Matt left the sea, unsure of his course.

He was working in a store in Washington, D.C.,

when a naval engineer named Robert E. Peary

came looking for a hat—and found an

   assistant besides.

Matt proved so able that Peary asked him to join

his next expedition to Greenland.

Soon Matt realized Peary's heart was set

   on one goal:

to be the first to stand at the top of the world.

But the Pole was not an easy prize,

and Peary and Matt had much to learn about the

harsh, cold north.

Matt studied with new teachers now: the Inuit.

Of all the explorers who entered their world,

Matt was their favorite,

and they gave him the nickname *Mahri-Pahlik*,

Matthew the Kind One.

"I have come to love these people. I know every man, woman, and child in their tribe. They are my friends and they regard me as theirs."

Matt took the time to listen,
to learn their language, and to make friends.
He studied how to build and drive a dog sledge,
and how to dress and hunt in order to survive.
Hard-working, skilled, and kind,
Matt Henson earned the respect of all.

"Eight days out and not a shot, not a sight of game, nothing. The night is coming quickly, the long months of darkness, of quiet and cold, that, in spite of my years of experience, I can never get used to..."

Through years of struggle and heartbreak,

the explorers faced

furious storms, the shifting ice,

and always, always,

the unrelenting, desperate cold.

On Peary's 1906 expedition, he and Matt

 set a record,

reaching farther north than anyone had before.

But storms forced them back,

the top of the world still out of reach,

nearly two hundred miles away.

"The wind would find the tiniest opening in our clothing and pierce us with the force of driving needles. Our hoods froze to our growing beards and when we halted we had to break away the ice that had been formed..."

Peary was determined to make one final try.

And so on July 6, 1908,

Peary's team of explorers set sail again

on the *Roosevelt*,

a ship so strong it could push through

the Arctic ice.

They spent the winter locked in the frozen sea,

readying sledges, supplies, food, stoves,

and more than two hundred dogs.

They hauled everything by dog sledge

to the northernmost tip of Ellesmere Island.

From this base camp they would launch

Peary's last attempt for the Pole.

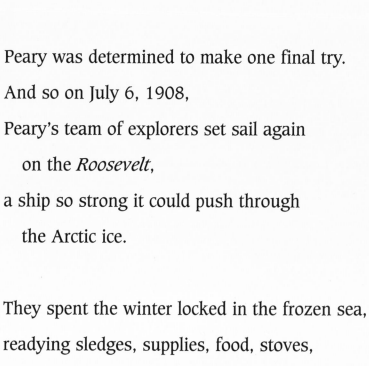

"The dogs were double-fed and we put a good meal inside ourselves before turning-in on the night of February 28, 1909. The next morning was to be our launching, and we went to sleep full of the thought of what was before us."

"Day and night were the same. My thoughts were on the going and getting forward, and on nothing else..."

"Traveling was slow, and the dogs became demons; at one time, sullen and stubborn; then wildly excited and savage..."

On March 1, 1909, Peary and Henson's team set out
across the frozen Polar Sea,
over endless ridges of sharp, drifting ice,
aiming for one point on the ice at the top of the world,
four hundred and thirteen miles away.
Peary's plan used support teams of men and dogs
to break trail, build igloos, and haul and cache supplies,
inching the assault forward day by day.

But there were only enough supplies for
one small team to make the fast and final dash
of five grueling marches,
one hundred thirty-three miles more.

By April 1, Peary had sent everyone back
except Matt and four Inuit men:
Ootah, Seegloo, Ooqueah, and Egingwah.

For Peary could not get along without Matt Henson,
experienced, resourceful, brave.
Matt was better than anyone else at driving the dogs,
fixing stoves and sledges,
breaking and finding the trail,
urging their Inuit companions on.
Without Matt Henson there would be no Pole.

"Without the Esquimo dog, the story of the North Pole, would remain untold; for human ingenuity has not yet devised any other means to overcome the obstacles of cold, storm, and ice that nature has placed in the way..."

On April 3,

as they moved across the ice,

Matt slipped and fell through!

Cold, killing water

closed over his head.

Matt could not grasp the edge of the ice

with his thick gloves.

"We were crossing a lane of moving ice...the block of ice I was using as a support slipped from underneath my feet, and before I knew it the sledge was out of my grasp, and I was floundering in the water of the lead."

Then, in a flash, strong Ootah was there.
He grabbed Matt and pulled him out
as if he were picking up a puppy by
　the scruff of its neck.
He tore off Matt's sealskin boots,
beat the water from his bearskin trousers,
saved the sledge and *Mahri-Pahluk's* life.

And then they simply kept on.

"From now on it was keep on going, and keep on—and we kept on; sometimes in the face of storms of wind and snow that it is impossible for you to imagine."

On April 6, 1909,

Peary planted a flag on a spot on the ice.

The Pole at last—or as close to it as they could figure.

After eighteen years, thousands of miles,

the thin, tattered flag they always carried

looked as ragged and worn as Peary and Matt.

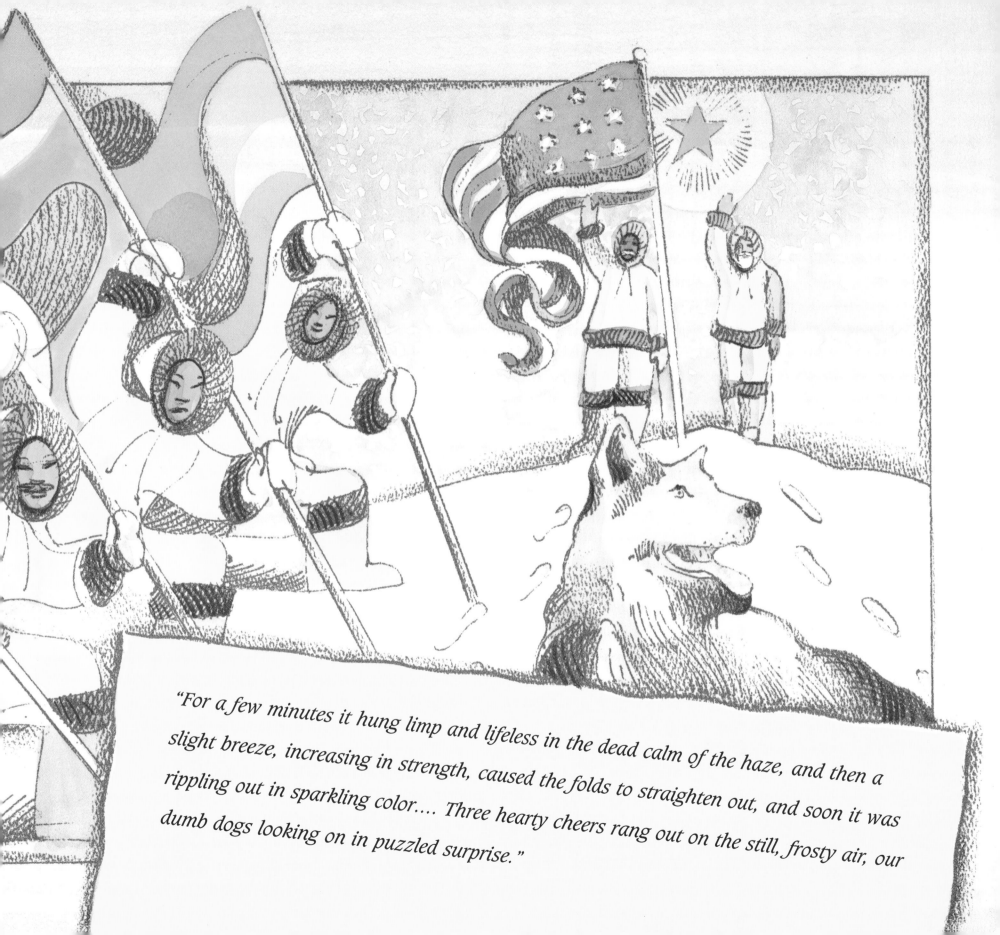

"For a few minutes it hung limp and lifeless in the dead calm of the haze, and then a slight breeze, increasing in strength, caused the folds to straighten out, and soon it was rippling out in sparkling color.... Three hearty cheers rang out on the still, frosty air, our dumb dogs looking on in puzzled surprise."

But now, at last,

these brave explorers

could watch it fly from the top of the world.

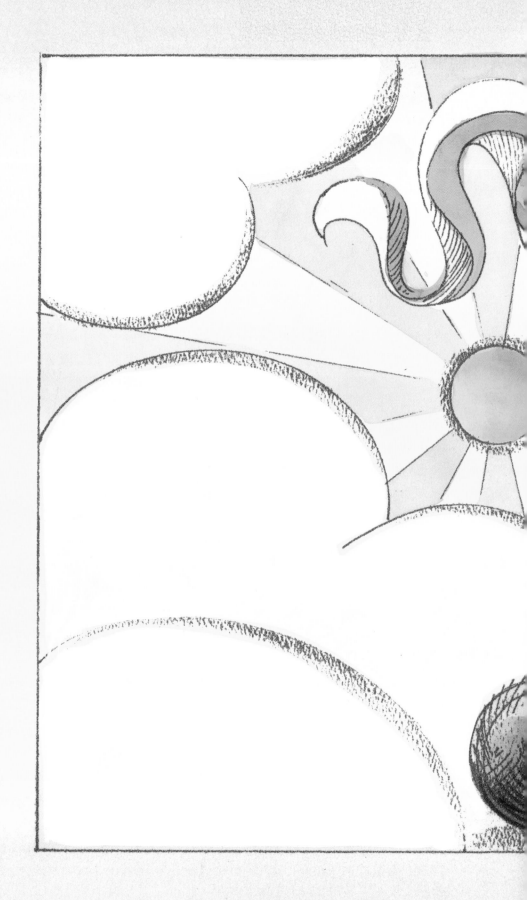

EXPLORE!

"The long trail was finished,
the work was done,
and there was only left for us to
return and tell the tale of the doing."

—MATTHEW HENSON

SOME YEARS AGO, when I first learned about the Arctic explorer, Matthew Henson I was surprised. Although I love to read about survival and exploration, I'd never heard of this extraordinary African-American explorer before. Even now, many people who recognize the name of Robert E. Peary are not familiar with Henson. Clearly, the racial climate at the time obscured Henson's unique role in the pair's success. Yet Matt Henson is an explorer to be admired, not just as Peary's long-time partner, but in his own right.

MATTHEW HENSON was a courageous explorer whose many skills and fluency in the Inuit language were absolutely essential to the success of Peary's expeditions. Born on August 8, 1866, Henson was orphaned at a young age and befriended by a sea captain who took him on as a cabin boy and gave him an education. Henson's wide-ranging talents became invaluable once he joined Robert E. Peary's Arctic expedition team. Henson fixed the sleds, hunted, and traded with the Inuit for needed furs and skins. Other explorers who went on the expedition recognized his crucial role, but the general public was slow to honor him, and upon his return from the Arctic, Henson had a hard time finding work.

Whether or not Peary and Henson reached the actual North Pole has been a matter of controversy since their return from their last expedition. Another explorer, Frederick Cook, claimed to have reached the Pole a year before them. Cook was eventually proved wrong, but arguments over whether Peary actually set foot on the Pole have continued. In 1990, in a study by the Navigation Foundation commissioned by the National Geographic Society, experts made an exhaustive examination of Peary's correspondence and navigational methods and concluded that on April 6, 1909, Peary, Henson, and their Inuit companions reached the near vicinity of the North Pole.

The fact that Matthew Henson's name is not widely known even today reveals much about the times in which he lived and the prejudices he faced. It was not until 1945 that the Navy finally awarded medals to the surviving members of the 1908–1909 Polar Expedition, including Henson. Other honors have followed; the U. S. Navy oceanographic survey ship, the USNS *Henson,* is named in his honor, and in 2000, the National Geographic Society posthumously awarded Matthew Henson the Hubbard Medal for exploration and discovery. Both Peary and Henson fathered children with Inuit women, and in 1987, Dr. S. Allen Counter, a Harvard professor and member of the Explorers Club, brought Henson's and Peary's sons on a visit to the U.S. to meet their American relatives.

In 1988, Henson and his wife were reinterred at Arlington National Cemetery, next to Peary, in large part through the efforts of Dr. S. Allen Counter.

MATT HENSON'S GRAVESTONE NOW READS:

MATTHEW ALEXANDER HENSON

CO-DISCOVERER OF THE NORTH POLE

AUGUST 8, 1866 — MARCH 9, 1955

"THE LURE OF THE ARCTIC IS TUGGING AT MY HEART.
TO ME THE TRAIL IS CALLING! THE OLD TRAIL-
THE TRAIL THAT IS ALWAYS NEW."

AND HIS BELOVED WIFE

LUCY ROSS HENSON

TIME LINE

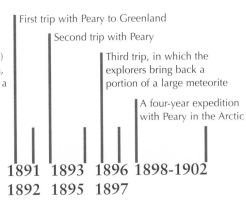
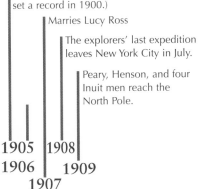

Born in Charles County, Maryland

Sails on the *Katie Hines*, where he is taught by Captain Childs

Accompanies Navy Civil Engineer Lt. Robert E. Peary (born May 6, 1856) to Nicaragua, to search for a possible site for a canal, later built in Panama

First trip with Peary to Greenland

Second trip with Peary

Third trip, in which the explorers bring back a portion of a large meteorite

A four-year expedition with Peary in the Arctic

The explorers get to within 175 miles of the Pole, setting a new record for going the farthest north. (They had previously set a record in 1900.)

Marries Lucy Ross

The explorers' last expedition leaves New York City in July.

Peary, Henson, and four Inuit men reach the North Pole.

1866   1879   1883   1887   1891   1893   1896   1898-1902   1905   1908
                                              1892   1895   1897   1906   1909
                                                                                                    1907

* Color blocks represent expeditions

There are many websites and books about Matthew Henson and Robert E. Peary.
To learn more, start your exploration at: *http://www.matthewhenson.com.*

Special thanks to Genevieve LeMoine of The Peary-Macmillan Arctic Museum and Arctic Studies Center at Bowdoin College for reading this manuscript. For more information about Arctic explorers see the museum's online exhibits: *http://www.bowdoin.edu/arctic-museum/index.shtml.*

Quotes are in Matthew Henson's own words, from A NEGRO EXPLORER AT THE NORTH POLE, published in 1912 and available as a free download from The Project Gutenberg. Release Date: March 28, 2007 [EBook #20923].

Other resources include DARK COMPANION: THE STORY OF MATTHEW HENSON

by Bradley Robinson with Matthew Henson.

New York: K. M. McBride, 1947. Revised Edition, 1975.

NORTH POLE LEGACY: BLACK, WHITE, AND ESKIMO

by S. Allen Counter.

Amherst: University of Massachusetts Press, 1991.

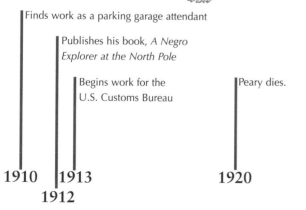

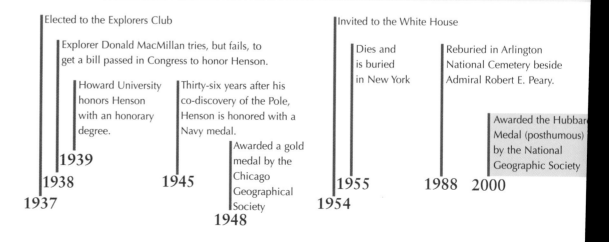

Finds work as a parking garage attendant

Publishes his book, *A Negro Explorer at the North Pole*

Begins work for the U.S. Customs Bureau

Peary dies.

Elected to the Explorers Club

Explorer Donald MacMillan tries, but fails, to get a bill passed in Congress to honor Henson.

Howard University honors Henson with an honorary degree.

Thirty-six years after his co-discovery of the Pole, Henson is honored with a Navy medal.

Awarded a gold medal by the Chicago Geographical Society

Invited to the White House

Dies and is buried in New York

Reburied in Arlington National Cemetery beside Admiral Robert E. Peary.

Awarded the Hubbard Medal (posthumous) by the National Geographic Society

1910 1913 1920   1939 1938 1945   1955 1988 2000
  1912   1937   1948 1954